MY BELOVED HAD A VINEYARD

MY BELOVED HAD A VINEYARD

Poems by Ryan Harper

THE POETRY PRESS

Los Angeles   Hollywood

THE POETRY PRESS

OF PRESS AMERICANA

americanpopularculture.com

Copyright © 2018

Americana and Ryan Harper

All rights reserved

Cover Art: *The Red Vineyards near Arles* by Vincent van Gogh (1888)

Library of Congress Cataloging-in-Publication Data

Names: Harper, Ryan P., author.
Title: My beloved had a vineyard : poems / by Ryan Harper.
Description: Los Angeles, Hollywood, [California] : The Poetry Press, [2018]
Identifiers: LCCN 2018002738 | ISBN 9780996777971
Subjects: LCSH: United States--Description and travel--Poetry. | United
States--Civilization--Poetry.
Classification: LCC PS3608.A7748 A6 2018 | DDC 811/.6--dc23
LC record available at https://lccn.loc.gov/2018002738

TABLE OF CONTENTS

I.

Nativity Scene on the Courthouse Lawn   1
A Heartland Neighborhood   3
Opening Our Eyes During Prayer,
   Tuesday Night Bible Study   4
Summerkill   7
The Gateway Arch   8
Hubble Creek   9
Cairo   15
Francesco on Black Friday   16
Country Gods   17
Blue-Eyed Devil on the Alpheus   19
American Beeches   21
Offender   23
code noir   34
On the Billy Graham Freeway   35

II.

Bradford Pears on the Church Grounds   37
Below the Line   38
The Feast of Saint Anthony   40
Passing Over   42
Mormon Boys Dancing to the
   Drummer in Prospect Park   44
The Psychic in Atlantic City   47
Experience at Princeton Junction   49
The Remains of Amelia Earhart   53
With a Banjo on My Knee   55

Panthera 56
The Discovery Center 57
Yemoja and Oshún: A Topography 59
The Order of Comediennes 62
Northwest of Terre Haute 64
The New Madrid Fault 67
Strangers' Gate 70

Acknowledgments 72
About the Author 74

I.

NATIVITY SCENE ON THE COURTHOUSE LAWN

So long since
I have heard
said the word
oxen;
what mechanics the word insists
upon stable faces—
what jaw, flexing caverns fleeting,
what imperial posture the industrious tongue
plodding the palate's ancient pasture,
steering and stopping a simple
breath into the landscape that is
oxen: a kind of grazing mammal.
Was it King James amplified
in a Christmas Eve
sermon, the annual delivery,
the dusty stock stacked
on wintry pallets?
for there was no room
for them in storage

At night alone the city turns them on,
those thin acrylic bodies,
a light bulb in each breast, their private shine
together a rotating agriculture
of the public sphere. I say the word
oxen, hear it said.
Joseph bows in time,
automatically, the baby kicks

and reaches for his mother, only
the sound, the low moan, of *oxen*.
        The scene is set
to a hidden metronome,
I gather—thirty beats per minute—
rum pa pum pum—for you see,
I am the marker of time—the dark watcher
who warms her hands over nativities
in motion, drawn to their faint heat,
their geared cadence,
the advent synchronized,
the return of *oxen*.

A HEARTLAND NEIGHBORHOOD

You can tell it's country because it used to be
an apple orchard, and there are a few here
who remember the orchard, and everyone
remembers it used to be an orchard.

The pavement, hardly seamed, used to being
empty, shaves the horizon bald—chalky
grids waffling hay-strewn lawns to be
mowed one day by first-time homeowners,
who you can tell are country because,
when they drive their loadless
pickups to the plant in the morning,
they lift three friendly fingers
off the steering wheel at any passing
sign of humanity, whistling to the song
on the radio, which you can tell is country
because someone in Nashville stroked once
the mane of a meowing steel guitar
deep in a studio booth loaded
with electric drums and gold records.

You can tell it's country because, at the end
of the day, people say "hello" at mailboxes
and "good-bye" as they waddle herniated
into a living room that you can tell is country
because the flat screen beams broad
as the bald horizon on a white wall, where hangs
a print of a painting of an apple orchard.

**OPENING OUR EYES DURING PRAYER,
TUESDAY NIGHT BIBLE STUDY**

We are caught in our early rising
from this circle
two thieves colliding on a rooftop of silent heads
still wide-eyed
we who love light rather than darkness
lifted up.
What seek we over this span
of skulls brought low,
Golgotha silence?

To look upon
faces praying as on French cathedrals—
lip tremors and hands wanting blood,
thigh-brushes swift as the death angel—
to catch
the ash-flakes of Sodom on our powdering tongues,
the face of Yahweh through his desert fingers?

How would that good apostle find us—
he whose midnight sermons
dropped dulled disciples like basin water
out upper room windows?
Would he who found life in a fallen sleeper
find it in two drugged awake
by the pious rondo of divine conversation?

How quickly surprise yields
delight bulbs your cheeks
you see me smile faithfully
you want to laugh
I want to
pour your laughter into this yawning space
so that we may run surely
ever over flat earth

and never again check our steps
almost tearful I sing in myself
the glory of moonlit heresies
perched atop these sunken temples
that they would ever sink
under our weight
that we would bury *amen*
alive
deep
true

But our quickened pulses slow
we grow eternally
familiar in seconds our secret marriage fades
and we lose each other among the muttered petitions
you drop your face

What have we conjured
in our rending ascension?
What do we see who possess vision
in this private chamber—
who speak no fire from heaven,
who freeze dumb just above
a ring of hearts swelling like loaves and the glow
of an approaching nightwalker's light?
What forked power raises us that does not hold?

What do we now
that we caught the other?
Should we walk out arm in arm
sobbing silently as to war
fall out and babble Pentecost,
take each other's blasphemy
for holiness, as happens from time to time?

Here is what we will do:
I will bow my head and count to ten
let you witness my submission
please
you must design grandly and bravely
upon what god brought me low again.
I will leave you to the seeing world
and pray that, after bible study,
you will tell me what you saw.

SUMMERKILL

Upon first discovering the bodies
by the hundreds—floating, rolling
upon the banks—we hypothesized
electricity: some lightning bolt; some
current ungrounded; some disconnected
wire; some ill-charged poachers.
But the conservation department
corrected us: summerkill. It happens
most like this: in shallow ponds;
during heat waves; when clouds
arrive; when algae die; where oxygen
dips; among carp and other
bottom-dwellers first. The stench goes
without saying. Going on nerve,
we of the neighborhood—who had
some high stake in the drafts—
began our ecological edit: in masks;
in gloves; with garbage
bags; high-stepping among
the schools of the dead
and dying. Not disposed
to waste a usable holocaust,
we sorted the field, scales
upon scales, into two
groups: those too long
gone for consumption; those soon
enough dead to be digested.

THE GATEWAY ARCH

A child of Missouri—
once someone told me
it was a serious
crime for aviators
to fly through.
Then there was that man

who parachuted
onto it: died—
awfully, I used
to think, recalling
how hot to the touch
was the silver metal

in the sun. Today
members of an elementary class
play on the lawn, between its legs,
running, passing east and west,

as each will. How high would
they have to leap before the Saint
Louis authorities
apprehended them?

HUBBLE CREEK

I.

Against parent wishes
I waded in currents too shallow most places to swim.

I couldn't swim
anyway. Hubble Creek: named before America's

transparent contact lens
hosted nebula and galaxies to coffee table

picture books;
we would look ourselves atomic ever after.
Farm runoff,

foamy horsehead clouds of cow piss berging the lentic
    surfaces—
I heard they

found polio in the water when they put samples
under scope.

Young, far-sighted, I had never seen polio. Apparently,
my parents had.

II.

Upstream: work
the slight squeeze toward the source—from my city of Jackson,

named after
a president, by Trail of Tears State Park, named after

objections,
to the town of Fruitland, named after no place which

I am aware of,
as the current sweeps behind my feet the kicked-up silt,
the life

my feet uproots: the crawdad shooting what eyes-on-the-prize
animals call

backward, the trust-fall propagation into dark crannies,
claws yanked straight

behind him on his tailstroke's kickback, watching with whatever
hind-vision crawdads

have former hidings
whirl to scrim. Leaving that, entering his other, he should

have been
a revolutionary creature—yielding balance, after fashions,

faithful glider
over mossbeds, provoked to brinks of fear, to new ledges.

But he is but
a brown and rosy crustacean—smart to go with old motions,
yes; smart, being

his own tailgunner, to fix on the historic destroyer
in retreat,

natural; but it takes unnatural and fatal turnings to inhabit
the fullness aside:

revolution: no backing in: the crawdad swims blind
to submerged roots.

III.

Or downstream:
mouthward, flush and culminate, self-collective—we

(younger, taller
friend and I) once walked I'll say two miles—farthest I had been,

though it was
at most times possible to estimate our general locus

by the higher
passages: bridges (pedestrian and otherwise), sirens,
signs, fences

of other friends' yards I knew usual days from patios.
This shit

gets deep in spots down here he said,
behind him Hubble's

voice running to accomplish itself; it would defeat
waders' purposes

of necessity suddenly
to be treading. I couldn't swim anyway. (But hell, Tom, warn't
romantical enough

to pay mind to cutbanks.)
They follow you down, the parts and particles you have been

moiling unto smoky
pillar. You walk in clouds, decomposing spirits diffusing

slower than murk
agglutinating. Always you are guessing about
steps and depths;

even shallows go opaque. My first walk
downstream alone

I stopped upon sighting a copperhead sunning on a rock.
Disturbed, it stirred

out of radiance, slid into the brume. I waited for effects to clear
before making new motion.

IV.

But I get ahead
of myself (git above my raisin'). In Missouri

a parent's aspired
hymns of resignation calk antiphonies like drift-

wood in flood;
they told me one June, following Hubble from Fruitland all

the way through
its swervings and mergers, I'd end in the Mississippi River—

each bleary mouth
another point source, docks on deltas on deltas until the Gulf
of Mexico.

Like many kids in Missouri in July I'd be driven
to Destin anyway.

Given eventual vacation, the known clarity
of sunshine state

waters lying at highway's end, why walk the creek?
A series of mouths

only, all the way down—that what I had my eye on?
(how do dat come, Huck?)

They said later
a faulty mirror caused the splendid ornaments of space

to blur under scope—
the first of forms spherical aberrations, as if the universe were
    fluid

and volatile.
A subsequent mission brought imposing fixture:

stabilizers:
the engineers plucked and hammered big physics

over the black
and nebular events. It cost the taxpayers,
lifting these

angelic professionals, gazing at gazings of the violent abyss,
(raisin' them

with this later raisin'). Immaterial—we would see clearly
the settled heavenly state;

heavenly hosts, repose the mirror, the self, the majesty.
Fix our eye.

But I get ahead of myself. Hubble ran between
my house and U.S.

Highway 61,
parallels expanding, bundling on occasion into singular vector
via two runoffs:
deluge, drunk driver—both native to Missouri.

For fair amounts
of time I lingered between the familiar linearities—

no direction, home
blurry through vine-linteled trees, across the shaded shallows.

No one believes
who hasn't seen that creek can reach the road in flood,
believes in traffic

fatalities, believes black holes contain such inward blast
as nullifies

all measures and scopes, all inward blasts. Crossing
my legs I sat

some great circles on the thin land—forced by virtue of being
between to seem

another current, line among lines, siting whim in the orders
of transparent contact.

CAIRO

At such points, every river
stinks, spread wide.
So don't blame the rivers,
the great flush of continents.
Have you not smelled yourself
in your brimming moments,
not swelled yourself as ideas
(the tangled menace of eroding shores)
roll out to a more substantial container—
at the delta point, *Dixie Mediterra*,
where you and your ancient stench
are vastest and most vanishing?

FRANCESCO ON BLACK FRIDAY

In the mall the light reaches almost all

a young man orbits his sunglass
kiosk, talking into the headcloud
of his hands-free device, dividing
apparent attention, his soft
gesticulating frame balloons convex
and pops in the chromatid rows
of designer lenses as he makes his passes,

the dense electric nimbus stirred

up into bluetoothed fragments.
Casual shopper, until you draw close
enough to believe otherwise, assume some-
body is in that cloud with him,
pulling him out of his overlit revolution
or plunging with him into it—
satellite of satellite of satellite.

What is outside the optic: dark matter

in heated exchange, infrared
splays of gravity implicit
against the food court quasar,
dim chiasma, round the spectacles.
Assume the young man and somebody
are working out their value:
a pair of shades repels the total light.

COUNTRY GODS

What makes the corncrops glad—standing reserve
the towhorse presses down the worm,
its glinting fuselage holds fast
against the unrowed weeds. Astride design

and incidental fallow, thinks the horse-
master, how negotiable
his ground for action: pitch it all,
upturn it, till it—toppling on itself—

yields, powers, brute and clean, so natural
direct objectors choke; at root,
the darnel is a weed, always.
Who would protest the hybrid plant? Would you

let out the endless trawl, resign to plumb
your life a breaking gulf, contract
beholden to the last debased
tormentor? Thinks the horsemaster, amount

over his plot, his work will never want
a proof: a prairie—*a priori*.
The decorated husband stamps
the surface, treading his own tracks, enlists

reserves in service of deployed reserves:
the blade of corn, the gassy vein,
the hidden fire and hinter flame,
the taut haulms skyward economically

collected for the final quarter. Thinks
the horsemaster, his tender crop
may be reeducated: graft
the younger branches, trim the older vines

(too routinized to whim; they love the earth
too much)—to cultivate alone
the usable resistance—breed
away what you are able. Clear the field;

to engineer the drought-resistant seed
is not to make it rain, yet lay
the mattocks to the earth's soft spots,
the sky will fall out of necessity.

Bugonia—the tested craft—the drone
of wings ascending from the rot
of chosen stock—engendered one,
ungendered, unbegotten—satisfied,

the five-star husband starts up to the big house,
lighter in his late entirety.
The horse snorts at one end of his rein,
flips the bridle, grinds the bit, and presses down.

BLUE-EYED DEVIL ON THE ALPHEUS

Lapping up light the gorge brooks
dim hope bears lingerers near
the steep lonely banks the boy
unconvinced of the virtue
of every onwardness, turns down.
Outside the gorge, the market
pursues—charges: the blue-eyed
boy pursues—discharges,
inside a hollowed innocence.
All is self-defense where all
is provocation: trading
games, women, hooded boys.

The good boy takes to the gorge—
under the Indian-bean trees'
broad hands his face turned to monitor
lizards, groundhogs, bears swaggering silty
through the undergrowth: moving moored,
putting on the dawn turns his spade
below his site—cleaving downward
in sublime blindness breaks through
arrowheads, routes his waters
to wash out the stable,
adapting his old stock, taking
interest, dawning in his gorge.

No longer able to stand
his ground because he cannot
imagine his way out
of necessity the good boy
disgorges—leaves
his goodness like an auger
upright in the earth
among the stiff reeds. Tick-ridden,
tanned, worked over with the dawn's

alien beams, scales the slope,
comes to market cloven, turns himself
in to an authority.

AMERICAN BEECHES

Walking with purpose to the wood's heart
I have come to consider the pure stand,
set off from the trailhead (so help me god,
I would have stayed). Through congeries
of maple and poplar, through purple flowers
oned-and-manyed into catkins,
through burs and knots of what will be
raspberries, I have come to assume the American
beeches in spectral, undifferentiated mode.
I would have stayed, so help me god.

Under the sawtooth canopy, off white barks tight
on trunks—flexed thighs—the light limes;
aglow in this tract I turn round
a single hulk and find carved
the initials: RH

under the knife the mirror of nature

What uses a species whose skin stays smooth
into old age—cotton-batted,
vivisected to a specimen:
unlobed planetree, eyeless aspen,
swabbed, flush for the marking,
cheap for the practicing omniscient—
hewed arbography, spanning
aureoles—arcade, catalogue,
reliquary of the sacred roundels?

Start and stop your measure at the sought
design and any stand is pure: the first
and last maples, outside by definition; measures
focused until even the lone American
beech dwelling elsewhere in the poplars
becomes an exclave; measures taken

until at last there is no elsewhere,
no exclave, only interruptions in the pure stand.
Again I turn round the notched hulk

What is this Titan that has possession of me

missionary of the alien work,
who after the uncircumferenced mandala
compresses properties beyond old native lines
dislocates the unmarkable growths.
What befalls the namer in the woods,

the marker of logs, who esthesic
and aching from a native fever
initializes a singular species: American
beech, surely related to European beech?
We can only say "the same" if we think difference
The day is getting on; the limelight bends—
yellow and green repartitioned in the deepening
shade. O Abendland, arcade
of the burnished hour, reclassify what you will:
considering the stand I take

leave among the maples and poplars,
burs and knots, a little embrowned;
I did not start here, by god—
I will stop again, marking the whole.

OFFENDER

"Now we know that whatever the law says, it speaks to those who are under the law"

I. No Golf Carts on Road

laughing all the way (Ha! Ha! Ha!)

Add a nametag and lanyard
to the polo shirt and khakis,
he could drive straight
into the White House.
These are quiet roads,
anyway; what does it matter
if he winds himself
through the courts and cul-de-sacs
innocent, forgiving as a children's
menu maze—and his children
so enjoy it:
oh what fun it is to dash
your way through settings
laid out specially for you—
to ride between the lines,
in the middle of the road.

II. Tables Are for Paying Customers

All the time she is here—
laptop, smartphone, bluetooth,
ornaments of remote investment,

charged and charging,
ranging one table today
(some days it is two),

absorbed, as I must seem,
in some distant call:
the art of looking badass
after the white fashion,
like someone who could sue,
write a devastating online review

I will take my business elsewhere
the great white threat:
to withhold what you never give.

Sudden cadenzas of stock quotes,
ultimatums, equivalences
that sound false this side of things:

tired snarls, no forte to them
but pressed enough for us to note
she will never note us until

Could you watch my things while
(Restroom Is for Paying Customers)
all the time she asks, all the time

I am partner to her crime—
so blunt, so easy; her things
yield less interest than she knows.

The barista rolls his eyes toward me,
one of his regular witnesses,
after she asks for another

glass of water (his eyes have this much
justice left). All the time I hear him
ask darker people to leave

who have clearer reasons to stay.
He does not ask her, nor I,
who orders all the time, and who will pay.

III. You Shall Love Your Neighbor as Yourself

where were you when peace broke out

inside a mall luminous
ferreting on frozen coffee
cursive caramel drizzles
easing by slurps into whipped cream
inside a good school
drug safe to calculus
pressed and trimmed
for the AP release
enough credit to turn you
into a sophomore

inside a hood with character
renewal's blackworked groundtroops
creating perimeters, pouring over
green parties of food tourists,
latest revival babel from the old
storefronts *for the best prosciutto
call not unclean what the lord hath made*

inside a sanctuary
brohood of the wounded hearts
full moon yawp of old adams
becoming new, delay
pedals, wahs too deep for words—
projection, submission, projection—
turned palms' slight stigma clawing ceiling-
ward toward confession without admission,
reeling toward the exit, across asphalt-

waving august earthlight uneasy
departures of the risen dead

I was there
prophesying peacemaker
in your name

IV. Do Not Feed the Wildlife

Some owed solitude,
some loneliness.
They meet awfully
much for balance:

born on a refuge,
a fire pit,
come so far by faith
or the worn paths,

some bodies begin
to take their best
ideas for solid
ground—to live feed

approach retreat site
surely, as you
would your own. All yours,
the refuge: paw

the hive, capture film
on tips—some come
to believe mortal
things: hands like these

extend charity
always, only.
Then it is finished.
Then some must die.

V. You Shall Love Your Neighbor as Yourself

Terrific stalagmitic drips
rowed sheer before
humming, flickering beams:
now sanctuary scored
open, alarming gallery
of the cased solvents;
now pit—deep densities fuel
the smallness, the awful
smallness of filled space,
jaundiced rings alight,
the gold cell shoots out,
turns inward

o for a total darkness to tame
the eyes' vast repertoires
of knowing: o for a thousand
tongues of fire to port
the cooling sponge through
the universe's furnaces,
annulling, in bold light,
if possible, even the elect-
-ricity, beyond hope, radiance.

Picture a cave, and
this is a white dwarf:
ghastly, blistering
node of lambent,

bursting skeins, exhausting
ancient vaults of power,
indulgent to its core,
stellar: remnant: dying:

VI. You Shall Not Kill

Austin Harrouff

unless there is no reason;
then it is art for art's sake:
high drama of high crime:

corpses, canvases, opportunities
for a performance piece.

So dexterous—do you even lift
a pound of flesh
or does it dislodge
itself from your media,
ascend to your mouth,
amass in the heroic
diet, as all lesser flesh?

Take them in: bloody cereal
of faces, on your face,
your blade, shocked
late before your resolve,
lost and open into
the higher opus.

Turn your eye to us,
this mordant moment
in the act,

take us in, your gagging patrons
who will deliver you,
try you after the fact:
the vitreous humor
in your smile reminds us
if you could explain it
you would not have to do it.

Like all of the greats
you hear and defy
the mad accusations
before they arrive,
dare us to detect
artificial substance
in your system
(we cannot)

Groaning, shaking
our heads as we must
before the Masters,
knowing truly
you are an ancient,
of Greek society,
we prepare a place for you—

we, the eyes of Columbos,
squinting, patting
your shoulder
as we take you in
as we must
as credits run

VII. All Dogs Must Be on Leash in Park

eighty-five percent
have not learned their lesson

    obeys basic commands

sorry sorry sorry
bells jingling,
sniffs a stranger's crotch,
tail stiffens, stranger draws in
don't worry he's friendly

    renders affection

overlights black
solitude that would cut
if we could withstand it
white despair; we are
not withstanding people

    does not snap

this is a dog-friendly space
who on earth does not like dogs

    takes discipline well

stranger later picked up
matches description
of unfriendly
sniffer of strangers,
bells jingling, locked up

    is good with other dogs

eighty-five percent one day
will learn what it means
to hold an empty leash,
saying *sorry sorry sorry*

VIII. You Shall Love Your Neighbor as Yourself

who would be greatest
works about bodies:

fastens to the far
and closing ones, loops

a bond slack, lets out
and takes in—one sweep

into the next broad
round of alignments

world blue consortiums
wax open, unsure:

constant deposits
of security:

demo: reviso:
losses, yours and ours,

greatest unfolding
unto body whole,

tending toward hope,
in hope, with hope.

Is this your homework,
who would be greatest?

IX. You Shall Not Kill

Rudy Eugene

unless there is no reason.
Black is a reason.

X. You Shall Not Kill

unless there is a reason:

The wells drained again
this summer—again
we are standing over holes
in the ground, and I know
that there are angles
hips can turn to make
heads look level
though the entire body
is cocked, the earth given
to slant: that one
an upright animal
given to decline,
one in running is made
suspect, one crawls
aggressively, one hoist
in mad repair, one
just cause he wanted,
one hoarse protest
from the pavement, head
open, slayed: all due force.
The body, a crook

in the neck, stands to reason:
as many can matter
as live—so few live.

code noir

> *Y'all know what a cipher is?*
> Erykah Badu

O that my words were now written! O that
They were printed in a book!
Instead: diacritics walking,
crescent moon bracketing,
catching select characters,
releasing by studied turn
the hoopoe in full delta span
over the crossroads. Instead:
the hailing figure, a fist
of hearty, enlarged peace,
knobby and coarse in the admitting dusk
—the clarity of light in retreat,
relief of a bullet-riddled land—
singing the body asiatic
above the burnt and burning timber,
scabbed and bleeding substance in occidence.
Instead: woman typing, mapping failures.
I have found out a thing
that thou apprehendest not
The writers of code
did not reckon the cipher much—
that behind the letter of the law
someone could make something else out.

ON THE BILLY GRAHAM FREEWAY

(One has precious
little assurance
in a rented vehicle)
Just as I am

arriving in Asheville
the engine starts going
all to hell
on me. Up here

everything is in between
big smoky other things;
Thus I grow disoriented. Thus

I grow anxious to right
the hot matter under
my hood: who has lodged
here in these

black mountains?
Chuck Olson? Or was it
Chuck Colson? It is
not easy to know

the traceries—so little
between them
each save the proclamation:

the will
to change, eternal conversion,
the breath—the consecrated
breath hot

down the slope
of my spine
even now I feel
(how these men

have driven me
to my end) Frantic as the dash-
board goes red
I find myself

addressing the great evangelist:
I know it is not
your typical method, holy
man of Pisgah, but I ask

for your intercession. Incline
that granite brow deep and wide
toward whatever
messiah you find lodged in

your black mountains.
Tell him you know
a lone driver taking your road
who requires assistance. Tell

him to look for a white coupe,
Texas plates (tell him it is a rental). Tell him
the driver, as always, did not opt for insurance.

II.

BRADFORD PEARS ON THE CHURCH GROUNDS

On the square the callery rows
you out a morning methodism—knocks
you back, the smell, spring likeness
of human and vegetable sex,
clubs you wholly, radiant pears
you did not plant like this—lovely most
unwanted pears, Bradfords, everywhere
invasive as grace's first laving,

read you prevenient through the late dews,
the public display: pears on pears
in peculiar, musky-white bloom
for weeks, then green as the rest,
lovely but for that bedsheet scent.
Easier to turn two eyes than one nose;
but on the naked square, inhaling
Wesleyan, it is all experience or not.

BELOW THE LINE

How the world can go flat fast
in fits and starts I do not know,
descending the Blue Ridge Escarpment,
falling water everywhere,
full with the daily deluge,
following the white bands off the cliffs,
to Dixie, end of gravity.

Under the weight of southern
summers we are walking
underwater, bearing the slow
and unrelenting tug backward,
without the icy refreshments
of the deep, the thrills
of drastic currents,
the grim satisfactions
of the desert way.

We compulsory amphibians
nod between silk-tree anemones,
through pods of columbine,
trout lilies, divers late blooms,
all things sprinkled, some immersed;
we the treaded submersibles
crawl on Bermuda grass,
groping into kudzu reefs.

You breathe differently down here.
You knew this in your own country,
but knowledge is one fragile thing;
with it you will not effect
the measure, the pace,
alone. There are faces
looking toward the sun here;
they are not the pale ones—

they the composite primes,
the chambered hulls hovering,
suspended in the sweaty brine,
contingent in thick solution,
studied in this specific heat—
what energy it takes to raise
a mass, even one degree:
depends upon the ratio of salt.

What lifts—surfaces—fathoms
the hoary stillness, necessary rot
at the base of the escarpment:
up and open-anchored, round
diluvian reaches I do not know
in what manner I will reascend
finally if I will reascend
I cannot rightly say.

THE FEAST OF SAINT ANTHONY

Much has been made
by certain theologians

of creation *ex nihilo*:

out of nothing   the thing   that makes   god

God. Indeed,

considering Behemoth   earth's expanse   straightly

this appears
weighty matter. Less,

though, said
of annilihation—

destruction *ad nihilo*—

which certain physicists
say (in their way)

is equally
divine:

un   imag   inable

for mortals. In truth,
I have heard

the whirlwind

darkening   westward

—in verse—

art   moving   everywhere

in space;
I know.

So at present
I am
uncertain

at a loss

as to who is listening
to my petition

when my keys
go missing.

PASSING OVER

I find no fault
on the sidewalks just
tall women mummified
in next year's designer
scarves cupping coffees
like caught frogs
Armani hobos and
the plastic spaceships
tethered scientifically
to their earlobes
whose minutes mean
more than crosswalk
signals gesturing wide
they could be talking
to anyone begging
anyone
for an acceptable
final quarter
years ago they would
have been arrested
or committed

there are lots of them
all not dirty not
ugly I am meeting Barbara
who is coming from the West
Windsor pilates class we are
going to the Latino film
screening and the lecture
on Argentinian Marxism
then I to the spired
library to read Alinsky
which is not due until next
week but my parents
are visiting this weekend

from Tennessee and I must be
ready to escort them down
the faultless sidewalks
and hear my mother talk about
how clean Princeton
is for being in New Jersey
and hear myself explain
why in such a populated area
it is perpetually necessary
to wash one's hands.

MORMON BOYS DANCING TO THE DRUMMER IN PROSPECT PARK

> *And it came to pass when they had arrived in the borders of the land of the Lamanites, that they separated themselves and departed one from another*
> Book of Mormon (Alma 17:13)

> *When I get mad I put it down on a pad—*
> *give ya something that ya never had*
> Chuck D

on mission every body
hear the drum and get wicked

if you believe that
celestial bodies gain and gain orbit
you might twist the oblique tendons of your core
along the open beat
as if it were a world
in cyclical
reform

you will believe this
the drummer with the most righteous chops
down the sacred grooves cast into the pocket
her flaming hammer strokes
rings of light
into loam

making record in the language of her father
displaced she moves you cry out
this maker will respond
outright things
in snarescape
spring

in stress of tom heads to the Eastern Park-
way my brethren to the East
note the Norway maple grows
in Brooklyn touching
tabouring on
invasive
heaven

to be sure idol worries matter
you make something divine the medium
in constant pulse in crease
immediately your base
comes unfastened

you must give it up
or turn it loose
outside time's wrenching roots
and boughs a sacred tree
grows ever resonating as we all play
after sounding motions soon we grow
fixed on the iron rods
that first drew out the cycling groove
even when the neophyte bands of wood cry out
for softer mallets

if you believe that
a tree of life will grow
an idol of necessity
even if the blessed No One hears the fall
and comes undone

you will believe this
matter will turn and tumble into holy whir
exceeding all the whiteness of phantom glory
you hear the drum you may as well
get wicked dancing in your developing world

THE PSYCHIC IN ATLANTIC CITY

As it was a late night this morning
I barely compose myself in time for clients
who do not arrive typically in winter
(little foot traffic)
whom I cannot help but expect nonetheless.

But I should admit I have seen warm spells
some Februaries of which the weathermen
gave no warning—a peek to imminent bloom
bringing masses to the walk. Such days I have counted
myself lucky I opened up despite the forecast.

As you are wondering, I should tell
you I know what they all think. Boardwalkers
are easy to read. What kind of sign,
a pointed finger? A step slowed two beats
per minute? Even the measured

gambler's gaze behind shades? I don't need your eyes
to know, buddy; I could make a fortune
on your kind any given day. It takes no
more than human sense. I know they laugh
at me, out of necessity; even my regulars

need read me a professional joker,
their patronage a teenager's haughty stroll
through an old funhouse—their enchantment now
their sneer before the bent mirror, the broken witch
in the shadows, their sigh their return to enchantment.

Sometimes I conjure justifications: I'd like to tell
them in all seriousness it's all play—
a free fall, a blush, dodge, and jitterbug;
the big tangle of lives I draw out
into knots—flash fictions,

fleshy nodes of meaning, small enough to fit
inside a palm, knots nonetheless; tell them
even full knowledge of the final sentence changes hardly
a boardwalker's direction, less the common ramble,
lesser the leaves, lesser their reader, lesser their composure.

But no one who comes to me wants my opinion.
Be it sorcery or grift, they want me in possession
of a system, not a hunch. It must be concrete.
It must give pleasure. Even the casinos seem empty
today. I wonder if I should have opened up.

EXPERIENCE AT PRINCETON JUNCTION

I thus express to work among the regulars—
who do not duck or grasp their looser properties
when earlier expresses zundle loud and hard
down the middle tracks
without notice
(excepting the doppler dialdown:
direct commuters flattening the very pitch
of trailing airs

from capital to capital, Union to Penn,
exceptions jarring ordinary air); among
the regulars—who never stand in consciousness
too near
the platform's edge
(sleeper cells, using and fusing
the northeast corridor's compact, well-joined
scheme). What is it

in me corresponds with them? Assuming the bent
gait of stock traders I am I guess one of them
after these years, waiting in measured motion for
my own express, on
the platform of our ordinary
lives, pacing often the same pavement,
aware of where the doors will open, where the seats
are likely empty—

well-suited, scrubbed, and licensed for these public cell
transactions. Corporate sighs, the clop and thrud of work
shoes—only the unbudded ears disaggregate;
only the ear
unbudded risks disintegration.
There was the morning when my train struck a woman.
Seated in the very front, I heard first the engineer's swelling
screams, as if he were steering his voice to roll back up the

doppler-dawn-dial-down, trying to prevent what he knew at once to be happening and to have already happened. It was an astronomically mad series of screams—as if to a thousand-year-dead celestial body that yet casts its thousand-year-old light into our present line of sight. I felt a knock so faint, a brake so slight, that but for the engineer's singular voice I would have thought nothing but ordinary delay. We the regulars looked up. The most regular offered first confirmation: *unfortunate, but ordinary during holiday time*. The conductor offered second confirmation: *there has been a casualty*. Timetables folded. I offered myself a final confirmation: *my express—causes—casual—ties*. I broke out in a cold sweat and became light-headed, in the heat of my spirit. Knowing myself in such events, I leaned against the window and allowed myself to black out. I awoke, after an unknown time, and felt stronger, as expected. I drank my water. And I looked and I saw the woman behind me sobbing softly; I could not catch her eye. Most were properly somber and silent—not visibly dismayed, foreheads hard and unmarked against the hard words that had passed through the conductor. I could not tell who grieved, exactly, or what grief taught them. They loaded us onto another train—a local, filled already with its own regulars. I could not tell what they knew, except that they had stopped, and we boarded, where there was no platform. By evening's commute, ordinary timetables had resumed.

There are crosswords among the regulars—prelude
to labor—to boarding, even: pre-commute, a self-
directed scrawl: parallel play: my morning ruined
before real motion
on the platform,
the brevity and levity
(reposing, filigreed remainders)
of *The Times*' riddles—

no characters aligning, vacant boxes, just
a single letter for one-down, and not a clue
about the puzzle's theme (whose knowing never helps,
occurring to me
always near
the resolve it would have hastened)
as my express approaches, I fold up
The Times to resume
shortly, at will. Not yet accustomed, fully, I

looked again and I saw something like
corded, living creatures, moving straight ahead, without
turning as they moved,
on wheels and wheels.

      Their appearance

      was like gleaming barrels,
          full of eyes.

The burning rail and wire—scorched
linearities—I cannot leave
my old associations:

beyond the narrow corridor, in empty, broad
Missouri, that stench always signaled something wrong
or wronging: paper by the radiator; dust
in the filter; some too-hasty conduct
of power-currents; ungrounded,
impartial energy consuming small,
incidental particles
of a nation caked in breakdown. Soon
      an inferno

As I looked I saw

          emerging beside the living creatures

other figures, each with the face
of a human being.

      When the living creatures stopped, they stopped,
          For the spirit of the living creatures

was in the figures.

the valleys of fires,
the earth the sign,
silty as the Mississippi's black
bottom, where rest
the channel cat,
long as men, against old tires,
discarded water heaters. I stand yet
am hurried

      feel myself burning in motion for all
          the figures of all this country.
      Morning by morning we wear another face—
          eagles and oxen.
      I cannot board today without noting
          the capital exceptions—
      inquest on the platform
          of the ordinary lives:

out of my longer vacancies, my monthly pass,
to realize my round world cloaked in linen
I thus express among the regulars a work
pressed for our revising
in our commute—
I shall be bound with them—I thus express
America—a daily motion—a crossword
I and you fill out in ink.

THE REMAINS OF AMELIA EARHART

It is not that I do not believe
in mystery. Just this morning I sat
blank and primitive under diurnal
shade, all recessive, nameless
the soft warming friction, dark on light.
Something untouchable blows overhead:
cloud of leaf imprintable;
the head is sensible to its effects.

It is that instead I believed
all uncompleted possibilities sealed;
we know all we would know
in time—the final stone had been thrown
into the final cave, the final ancient scrolls
procured, all that remained, translation. Having flown
in the sun longer than the sphinx,
we knew all we would not know,
wise to being none the wiser, never.

So when they found personal effects—
freckle removal cream (her natural weakness;
no one knew upon her vanishing
she still anointed herself with vanishing)
a woman's shoe, the tobacco her navigator
preferred—the difficult article of faith was not
Amelia is found but *Amelia, so long
visible, just now has been found*

What does such an article mean
for the man of panoptic faith—the man
of global positioning, astrology finally turned over,
the sky's chart of the earth compass-marked,
fashioned with planes and satellites
and silicon seerstones; the man of commissioned
soldiers looking grainy-green through night vision

goggles into the desert for enemies of his state;
the man of all healings' eventuality, looking grainy-green
at the golden tablature of toxicology reports,
at men as Christmas trees walking; the man of wide,
ballistic, compassionate precision; the man
of universal application, the phrenological sweep
of his finger across his handheld screen,
divining his world no bigger than a hazelnut?
Is not this thing in my right hand

All that can be seen has been should
be seen. Saint Anthony lies dead
on some island—doesn't he? Pray

tell, Amelia: How long after the crash
must a grounded flying woman hold
her personal effects before the sun
or lesser searchlights bleach articles
to artifacts to facts to nothing? Why
has this your atlas been so difficult
for searching men in searchable times?
Why have men searched for you,
the lost lady adventurer, like a city
of gold from whom the blemishes
like darkened pixels have vanished? Whose pacific
tide fogs your landing strip? Whose the right
of way? What kind of faith is yours,
blessed Saint Amelia, your pacific
elusion of god knows
how many flyovers since yours
the most visible vanishing—yours the lesson
in instrumental failure, yours the call
to the man of panoptic faith
to consider new articles and become
newly sensible to the inconclusive?

WITH A BANJO ON MY KNEE

America the resonating chamber:
the bearded open-backs claw
and hammer up every high hill,
under every green tree, their graduated
volume up blessed St. Elias,
Denali (for tribute) fifty to the Wind Cave
of the sound of the small voice;
America: the wood laid in order
by the great father holding the scalpel
to his neurasthenic son's neck—
whole head sick, whole heart faint
with this mysterious floating,
the great white fleet fleeing the great
white city, taking west-
ward to heal the new nervousness
of the open back—west without
presence, house, field—for a time,
alone, encamped. All should return once
graduated from the high places
and offer their singular vistas up
in photo shares; it comes natural,
the pluck, strum, and *drang*. America:
this is the age of open-backs
ever requiring external
amplification

PANTHERA

Washington, D.C., January 2017

They said he had been playing
with the lion again:
tussle, long cravat and tail
before the wide mouth,
rolling in the open court,
someone someone's toy,
growling and growling back,
playing alpha, playing king—

They, Lion—a full jowl,
in the main a golden thing.
But the mimic alone
chasing likeness falls
headlong into his game,
alone in the roar
of singularity,
lost when the objects change.

Witnesses would have heard
claw and cuff screech against marble.
What possesses a man
that he lionize himself
before his animal?
What came over him
when the animal
began to play fair?

THE DISCOVERY CENTER

Before the presentation, we fumble through learning
stations, juggling orbs, knotting the Pleiades into tinkling
catkins, spinning the parabolic, pretending generation
of weightlessness, awaiting someone
else's closing word. What are we that we
are mindful of the mockup, the scale
model, that we lead our children on
the interactive game, the weekend make-believe:
wrists turn worlds turn?

Then the presentation in full theater: stain-
master carpet, cello synth pad dozing
mystic into deep laboratory tissue,
a long-digited voice, breathy with retreating
omniscience, talking us through projections: novas,
white dwarves, red shifts. *This is what our universe
was like long ago; the archaeologists call it
Age of Major Tom and Ground Control.
Its light just now is reaching us. Just now we are
beginning to comprehend the expanse. Amazing,
is it not, to peer into origins?* Ponder
a going otherwise, imagine the long attraction
of what did not have to be—but a stray neutrino,
slight break in carbon cycle, Center trustees
choosing tile over Stainmaster,
female over male

narrator—of course these are unaccountable
formations of the material at hand:
so what, the fretting oracular across
flagged moons, trunkless Kilroy's signature
painted over in spumatic fits of passing repair,
ever the mobile home that the builders rejected
shuttling fancy and subjunctive the bit-digited
dismantlers, for the millionth time, to forage

through the next wreckage, to gut-wrench the copper
in the condemned smithy—unaccountable,
how the white dwarves yank clear
the verdigris stock,

the last blue shift. The presentation ends
with running credits. Half the letters
in the exit sign light up; deducing the remainder,
we file out of the center to hall, lobby,
portico, deck, allow our irises and noses to contract
under ultraviolet day. We sail home through the cityway,
recalling lyrics unmoored from metronomic
orchestration. But for the small bangs
of our heads against the windows—irregular
and constant as the warped causeway below us
(no eye can see, no one in motion cannot but feel
the ruts) —we hum lines, out of time:
planet earth is blue and there's nothing I can do.

YEMOJA AND OSHÚN: A TOPOGRAPHY

Leaving our devices
so high we only catch sight
of them against the open nights

moving in their way
cross fixed courses
we are seen in turns

in our clear days:
satellite gaze returns—
returns not mutual.

Landsat delivers us
in high definition
aerials of the waters meeting:

delta: blues
and yellows, cloaks rolling
down from Our Ladies' crowns

delta: rates change
cross alluvial shallows
subaqueous plains

delta: symmetry
of lava flows above
ancient sea floors

delta: Rose
of Ammon, tent
of Moloch, pillar of salt

delta: marks *la place*,
points of difference
inside old equations

delta: a pace,
a form of release
from forms

delta: Landsat—
such gliding wonders!
what wondrous triangles!

A continent's abstract algebra
in elementary relief,
the fluvial flange of filaments

spits in a body numinous
as words—lines, surely projective:
real or complex, difficult

to tell even in the high contrast
of a false color
image—delivers us

a state between
the origin and
the end, between

the river and ocean
spirits embracing,
clashing, converging:

patakís meandering,
oxbow, old streams
buckle to latest unions—

daughters, sisters,
lovers, grasped in aerials—
we so remotely sense
becoming subjects
in full dissolution,
according to our devices.

THE ORDER OF COMEDIENNES

Form is boundlessness; boundlessness is form.
                from The Heart Sutra

this is where
she finds herself:

first rule of improv:
wild monastic

monky mind imp-
roves a scene

with a sprawling eye—
pupil of what was,

pupil after the end-
less gestation

of new states,
openly orthodox,

cardinal as a minute
hand in her will

to change—the eye ever
after surprise

and permanence
at once—that eye only

can fall short:
there's the comedy.

It takes wild patience,
oblate discipline,

to complete, be completed—
she leaves room ahead

of herself for you;
if you can,

improve the scene
for another...

NORTHWEST OF TERRE HAUTE

It is really midday; we imagine
it is round midnight—better illustrates
our points: how we two rode off
together, different hours from our native Missouri,

you stand in Indiana, I in Illinois;
we are aware of a theoried figure between us,
dividing states and time zones
alike: politically, mathematically
necessary but insensible—

what are lines but overextended points—
we stand alone on neither, just
encompass them, complete with them.

In a high country, dreams stay with you:
easy our gaze commutes the zones;
easy in the Indiana summer your tones
permit your open passing for a member
of any tribe not your own.

What peace to dwell here:
things hold well, here
above Birdseye—well, here below Hebron,
the Wabash rolls far today,
easy: turn the dial, ten steps, either way

to approach and speak, together, draw near—
the shorter dwellers here

must make mental conversions all
the time—too late or too early

for some neighbors to gather. Draw near:
our instruments strain too precisely
to bind town to town. Once they seemed up to it,
but power lines do not make these conjunct—
nothing rightly soldered overhead,
along these roads, wobbliness born.
I decline to turn the dial

at this time—the unified field is a nightmare. First we must
imagine better breaks in the plains, in the spectral middle
states; mark the geographs in spicatto geologues; with
winnowing forks pitch and comb musical staffs in the annotated
dust. We must invent better rotations, higher scores, love, an
unlikely interval, cover crop outlines in the unmeasured earth,
inscribe circles of fourths. I'm sorry we cannot connect our calls
at this time. These are the breaks.

But hope departs from hearts of harder dwelling:
listen to the jingle, the ghost train's rumble,
its phantom draft splitting the night,
descending the flowery mountain, cutting the whole

fog. Even if they cannot bring us nearer
we know our words as diaphones.
Hope's departing is a running over—
diatomaceous flourishes far under
Prophetstown, where open-mouthed
Tippecanoe rolls into Wabash—
pure white, pure Shawnee, joining, forking—what

are streams but overextended drops—
the water has moved, but our feet stand
on its deposit; underground the limestone
keeps the ancient seams, its calcic
brokenness, the resembling difference between
sediment and sentiment. Secession

mid-nation hurts the most; our border
words will sing us out of dimensions
though we cannot sing ourselves.
Mount up below the theoried line,
above the theoried plain—follow me
and I will make you fissures
that you might consecrate a stranger whole.
The central man pretending midnight
appealing to the future: looking toward eastern standard,
midday from yesterday, imagine me
seeing raised a victor—stranger—friend—
I know as well as not my own.

THE NEW MADRID FAULT

No land's end. Not hardly the gravelly
vapor of glacier-dragged natural borders,
no standing and staring steam-eyed
at the agnostic sea, wondering
if that sand-pawing rolling leveler might
send toppling across the waterline, headfirst
and angry onto the beach, one of creation's
unknown, unanswerable monsters,
or if the monster at last is a flatlined
horizon falsely rouged and stuffed—
the sky's criminal undertaking: oceanic
taxidermy.
                      No,
                                  the landlocked
have no privilege of being
taken under by coastal melodramas—tides,
plate tectonics, sisyphian
shape-shifting, the crawl of continents
wrinkling, buckling one against another.

But we have stood on edges of a kind,

and we have learned lessons lugging
ourselves atop this protean soil
in a double-breasted nation: Missouri:
a slave state ever pledged to a civil union
ever pledged to the feasible eradication
of slave states, where legislative compromises
protecting peculiar sacred institutions break,
sorrowfully, predictably, where solid fugitives
queer and dark cannot exist because
there is no homeland unquaked, neither
a river that will not, under collusions
of certain seismic lunacies, run
against itself, insinuating with genesis

immediacy new lakes, islands, cotton fields,
family dwellings

—Remember this, fringe Americans—
        that we have learned lessons also

from the flam of hail on cars,
the quiet order of floodplains, the storm
sirens whining entirely into boiling green
skies, the fool's gold buried
under exit ramp real estate, the jet exhaust
smeared like whiteout above and beyond
farms that we know look empty
to pilots and conference attendees,
network news, K-12 curricula,
zoning laws.

        The fiction of the edges occurs to us—
          a littoral transcription
sitting fidgety on our place.
So we have choices.

Some occupy pews and restaurant booths
to wait for the high resolution in the bill,
munching out of habit the complimentary
communal bread as servers back platter-handed
through swinging double doors. Some keep
notebooks, where the paradoxes paged
and clasped work themselves out
as theology, poetry, grocery lists,
vaccination records. Some keep gardens.
Some hang seaside images (Leviathan
drawn and hooked) on hallway plaster,
foggy in the ribbed clouds
of room shufflers' peripheral vision,
sleepers in corridors descending deep
into the subdivision night chambers

of modular interior castles,
no edges, no fringes,
no ends in sight—even our own.

STRANGERS' GATE

Of late this has been my entry:
Manhattan Valley, rolling, the sweep,
sidewalk hexes popping under root flex,
hard breaks in three dimensions,
under the long stairs,
abiding in the stranger
rock formations—native, by design,
law. Frederick, your condition:
exalt your valley without exposing it
to the loneliness of the high places.

I have met them as the day recedes
riverside, under your eye, Frederick—
on the corner, the gossip of angels
on worn benches. Parkside we muse
with our bodies on suffrage,
the experiment of real
relation: Yankee cap,
heavy stroller rolled up the ramp
into the park's northern heart
where we grandchildren of the south
gather. We work through each other
some strain of common life
in the chops of city passage,
a little mad for contact,
a little without it, closing on.

At twilight we idle, Frederick—
some take on legato as call
in the midst of the bowed
heads punching through time
toward the crests of silver
and gold—theirs, not the pose
of the gate, opening before
round hostels and dwellers
in the valley. Frederick,
such as we have we give
over to the other in the gate,
the entry where stranger
meets stranger, of late
our only entry.

ACKNOWLEDGMENTS

Grateful acknowledgment to the following publications, where the corresponding poems first appeared:

Alligator Juniper: "Yemoja and Oshún: A Topography"

American Journal of Poetry: "Offender"

Adanna: "The Psychic in Atlantic City"

Appalachian Heritage: "Nativity Scene on the Courthouse Lawn"

The Appendix: "The Remains of Amelia Earhart"

Berkeley Poetry Review: "Hubble Creek"

Big River Poetry Review: "Summerkill"

Broad River Review: "A Heartland Neighborhood"

cahoodaloodaling: "Below the Line"

Chaffin Journal: "Passing Over"

Cimarron Review: "Bradford Pears on the Church Grounds," "The Order of Comediennes," and "Panthera"

Episodic: "Experience at Princeton Junction"

Kestrel: "Country Gods"

The Litchfield Review: "Opening Our Eyes During Prayer, Tuesday Night Bible Study"

Mississippi Review: "Francesco on Black Friday"

Nassau Review: "The Discovery Center"

Plum Tree Tavern: "American Beeches"

Potomac Review: "Cairo"

Review Americana: "Mormon Boys Dancing to the Drummer in Prospect Park" and "The New Madrid Fault"

Still: "On the Billy Graham Freeway"

Sugar House Review: "The Feast of Saint Anthony"

Whirlwind Magazine: *"code noir"*

W.B. Yeats Society of New York: "Strangers' Gate"

ABOUT THE AUTHOR

Ryan Harper is a visiting assistant professor in New York University's Religious Studies Program. He is the author of *The Gaithers and Southern Gospel: Homecoming in the Twenty-First Century* (University Press of Mississippi, 2017), and the poetry chapbook, *Memphis Left at Cairo* (Finishing Line Press, 2013). His writing has appeared in the *American Journal of Poetry*, *Chattahoochee Review*, *Review Americana*, *Huffington Post*, *Killing the Buddha*, and elsewhere. A native of southeast Missouri, Ryan lives in New York City.

www.ingramcontent.com/pod-product-compliance
Lightning Source LLC
Chambersburg PA
CBHW020951090426
42736CB00010B/1362